The Workbook

for

The Circle of Fifths:
visual tools for musicians

Volume 2

Substitute dominants, progressions, major harmony

Philip Jackson

The Workbook: Volume 2 – Further Steps

A workbook for *The Circle of Fifths*

Book 3 in the series : *Visual Tools for Musicians*

v.1

ISBN: 9798744147112

Preface

While working with young musicians, young in both the sense of experience as well as age, I quickly saw the help that could be made in their progress if we used their visual memory as well as their aural memory. I published *The Circle of Fifths : visual tools for musicians* and this has proved to be a very useful addition to teaching materials. I have used these tools for teaching classes on music theory and in practical sessions with improvising musicians. The handouts I made for practice have also evolved with time and these proved very popular as well as useful.

Practical teaching experience showed that students could benefit from further examples to help them practice and acquire the habits necessary to enhance their visual memory. This was confirmed by requests from the students themselves. Thus, it came about that I decided a workbook companion to *The Circle of Fifths* would probably fit the bill most appropriately.

Once I was well into the preparation of the exercises, it became clear that the work was too extensive to go into a single workbook. I didn't want the resulting workbook to become a doorstop but I didn't want to cut the exercises short. The result was that the workbook appears in three volumes. This second Volume covers chapters 8, 9, 10 and that part of 11 dealing with the major scale in *The Circle of Fifths*, and follows the same chapter numbering.

Volume 1, *Early Steps*, provides practical work covering chapters 1 through 7 of *The Circle of Fifths*. Volume 3 treats the minor harmony aspects of chapter 11 as well as chapters 12 and 13, quartal harmony and transposing instruments.

Nothing stops musicians from playing, composing and listening to music without the slightest knowledge of the theory behind that music. In fact, such theory as exists should not be taken as rules so rigid that if broken the universe will crumble. At best, theory only codifies the accepted practice of the period in which it is written and it has never ceased to evolve.

My firm belief is that progress arrives from understanding and that education is the way to improve understanding. The present volume is the result of years of experience with students and has proved helpful in speeding up their endeavors to improve their practical approach to music. I hope that you too will find it of assistance.

I welcome readers' comments and suggestions which may be addressed to me by email :

support@le-theron.com

Philip Jackson, 2023

Table of Contents

PART 1

Exercises

Volume 2

Introduction

I have followed essentially the same layout, order and treatment of the different uses of the circle and readers of *The Circle of Fifths* should be able to follow and practice these uses as they proceed chapter by chapter.

This volume is divided into two parts. Part 1 provides the exercises and Part 2 provides the answers. In Part 2, I have provided some additional discussion where I felt it could be useful to enhance understanding. One of the best aides to enhancing your visual memory will be to follow the discussion details closely on the circle diagram associated with each answer. This will help imprint the patterns especially of chords and progressions and will speed up your work with visualization.

Please note that the numbering of the Exercises follows the numbering of the chapters concerned in *The Circle of Fifths*. Thus, you should find it easier to reference the material covered by the Exercises.

The resources section has a link to some additional material which can be downloaded if you wish.

Conventions regarding chords

I have maintained the conventions used in *The Circle of Fifths* and these are shown below.

Triads with perfect fifths

- The perfect major triad will be represented simply by the letter name of the root note. C major triad will be simply written as C.

- Minor triads will be represented like this : Cm

Triads with altered fifths

- Augmented triads will be represented as : Caug

- Diminished triads will be represented as : Cdim

Seventh chords with perfect fifths

- Major seventh chords will be represented like this : Cmaj7, C△

- Dominant seventh chords will be shown as : C7

- Minor seventh chords : Cm7

- The minor triad with major seventh : Cm.maj7

Seventh chords with altered fifths

- the augmented triad with major seventh : Caug.maj7, Cmaj7#5 , C△#5

- the augmented triad with minor seventh (altered chords) : C7#5

- the half-diminished seventh : CØ or as Cm7b5

- the diminished seventh : Cdim7

Conventions regarding scales

We shall use the major scale as the point of reference for all scales and modes and for harmonic analysis, the degrees of the major scale will be represented by Roman Numerals using upper case to represent notes having a diatonic major third and lower case for notes having a diatonic minor third.

Melodic analysis

When deriving a chord or another scale, we shall respect the convention of using as the point of departure the major scale commencing with the same tonic note name. In this case, we shall use Arabic numerals.

8 - Substitute Dominants

Tritone Substitution

Following on from the exercises in determining notes a tritone apart in Chapter 6, we can now apply this knowledge to the practical use of tritone substitution in ii–V7–I (2-5-1) chord progressions. It is the tritone contained within the dominant 7th chord that provides the instability which in turn provides the motor for progression to the resolution provided by the tonic (I) chord. This chapter provides exercises on the material in Chapter 8 of *The Circle of Fifths* and the exercises are numbered accordingly.

Two dominant seventh chords with their roots a tritone apart will contain the same tritone interval, albeit inverted in one of them. And as we know, an inverted tritone remains a tritone.

For example, the G7 chord is formed of the notes G B D F. G is the root and the tritone is formed between B, the 3rd, and F the 7th. The note a tritone away from G is Db. If we form a dominant 7th on the root Db, we get the chord Db F Ab Cb where we again find the tritone F - B (enharmonic respelling of Cb).

So, if we can quickly find the root note a tritone away from the root of the V7 chord, we can vary the sound of the progression while maintaining its momentum.

We also get a chromatic progression. ii–V–I becomes ii–bii–I or Dmi7–G7–C becomes Dmi7–Db7–C.

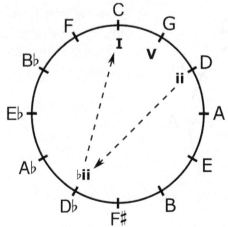

Figure 8.1: a chromatic ii–V–I

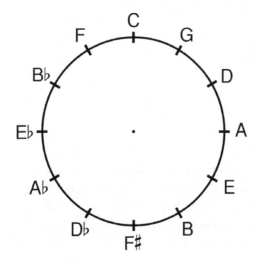

Exercise 8.1: Draw the chromatic progression resulting from substituting the dominant 7th in a ii–V–I progression starting at Ami7 and name the chords.

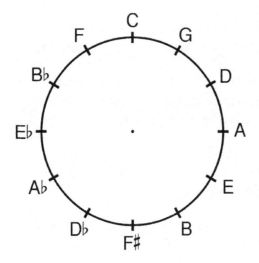

Exercise 8.2: Draw the chromatic progression resulting from substituting the dominant 7th in a ii–V–I progression starting at Emi7 and name the chords.

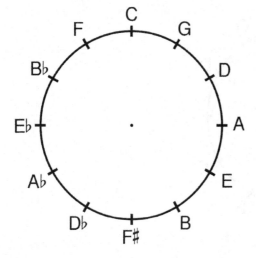

Exercise 8.3: Draw the chromatic progression resulting from substituting the dominant 7th in a ii–V–I progression starting at Bbmi7 and name the chords.

Exercise 8.4: Draw the chromatic progression resulting from substituting the dominant 7th in a ii–V7–I progression starting at Fmi7 and name the chords.

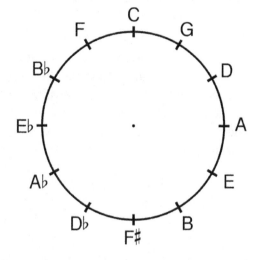

Exercise 8.5: Draw the chromatic progression resulting from substituting the dominant 7th in a ii–V–I progression starting at F#mi7 and name the chords.

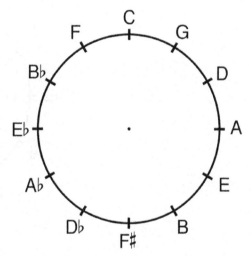

Exercise 8.6: Draw the chromatic progression resulting from substituting the dominant 7th in a ii–V–I progression starting at Abmi7 and name the chords.

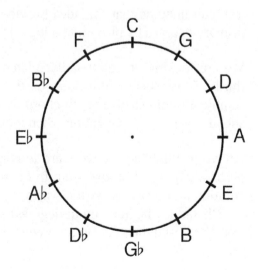

Bartok Substitutions

Bela Bartok extended the notion of harmonic functions of the principal degrees of the scale, the tonic, sub-dominant and dominant, to the other degrees. Each of the three secondary degrees was likened in functionality to a primary degree a minor third above. Thus the second degree was likened to the sub-dominant, the third degree to the dominant and the sixth degree to the tonic. The seventh degree was then likened to the second, again a minor third above and the remaining notes of the twelve in the chromatic scale were similarly associated with notes a minor third away.

This gave musicians a situation as shown in the following image which uses as an example, the C Major scale:

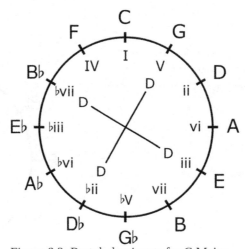

Figure 8.2: Bartok dominants for C Major

You can imagine that this idea provides multiple opportunities for substitution of any of the primary degrees by providing a logic for expansion of the tonality into other regions.

We are looking at functionally related tonalities with all like functions separated by minor thirds. These sets of four notes on the circle are not chords of the tonality although they resemble a diminished seventh chord in their structure. In practical terms we can treat them as such for ease of visualization when looking for additional substitute dominants.

Above in this chapter, we were looking for the tritone substitution which would give us a chromatic ii–bii–I progression. In the image above for C Major this would be the G–Db substitution and this was Bartok's primary axis (degrees V and bii). His secondary axis contains the Bb and E (the bvii and iii degrees) as possible dominant substitutions. The E (degree iii) is less often used than the Bb (degree bvii) but remains a possible variant.

Exercise 8.7: Mark the Bartok dominants and label their degrees for A Major tonality.

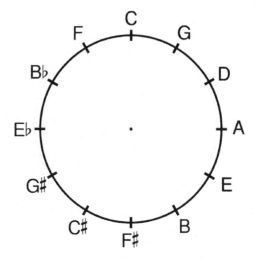

Exercise 8.8: Mark the Bartok dominants and label their degrees for F Major tonality.

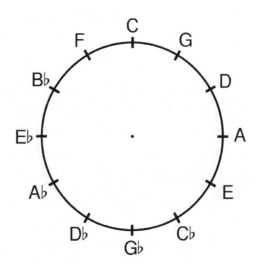

Exercise 8.9: Mark the Bartok dominants and label their degrees for Eb Major tonality.

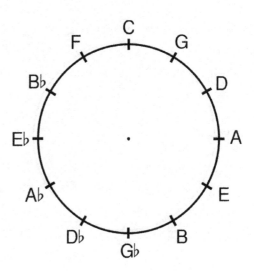

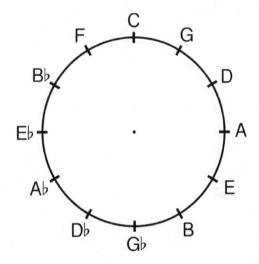

Exercise 8.10: Mark the Bartok dominants and label their degrees for Db Major tonality.

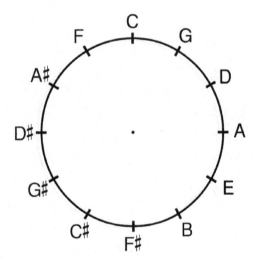

Exercise 8.11: Mark the Bartok dominants and label their degrees for B Major tonality.

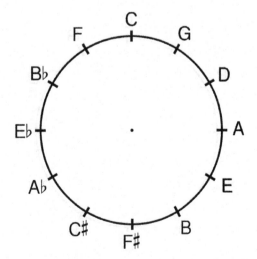

Exercise 8.12: Mark the Bartok dominants and label their degrees for D Major tonality.

9 - Chord Progressions

In this section, we shall present some exercises on common chord progressions following what was presented in Chapter 9 of *The Circle of Fifths*. Some of the most powerful progressions are based on descents of an interval of a perfect fifth. This is ideal for visualizing on our circle of fifths.

The 2 5 1 or ii–V–I progression

This is perhaps the most well known as well as one of the simplest progressions.

Exercise 9.1: Draw on the circle of fifths the ii–V–I progression in the key of D Major. Name the chords involved and their nature.

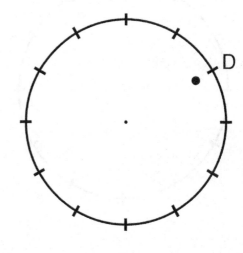

Exercise 9.2: Draw on the circle of fifths the ii–V–I progression in the key of Bb Major.– Name the chords involved and their nature.

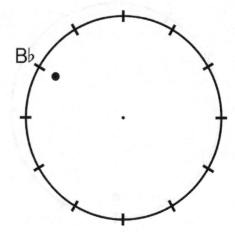

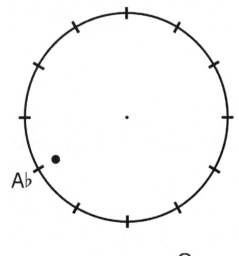

Exercise 9.3: Draw on the circle of fifths the ii–V–I progression in the key of Ab Major. Name the chords involved and their nature.

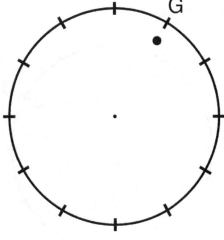

Exercise 9.4: Draw on the circle of fifths the ii–V–I progression in the key of G Major. Name the chords involved and their nature.

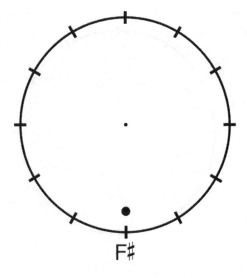

Exercise 9.5: Draw on the circle of fifths the ii–V–I progression in the key of F# Major. Name the chords involved and their nature.

Now try a few minor keys. Minor harmony is richer and varied because of the several alternatives but for the next few examples we shall assume the **harmonic** minor key.

Exercise 9.6: Draw on the circle of fifths the ii–V–I progression in the key of F minor. Name the chords involved and their nature.

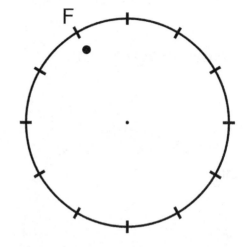

Exercise 9.7: Draw on the circle of fifths the ii–V–I progression in the key of Eb minor. Name the chords involved and their nature.

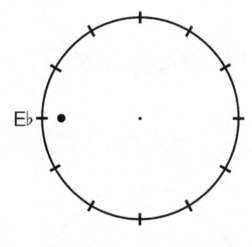

Exercise 9.8: Draw on the circle of fifths the ii–V–I progression in the key of B minor. Name the chords involved and their nature.

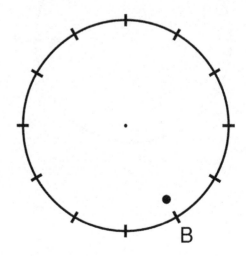

The next exercises are a mixed bunch all in the major scales.

Other progressions

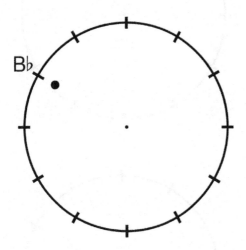

Exercise 9.9: Draw on the circle of fifths the vi–ii–V–I progression in the key of Bb Major. Name the chords involved and their nature.

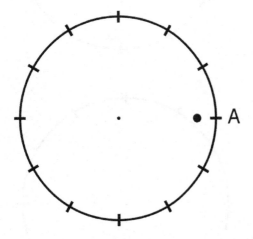

Exercise 9.10: Draw on the circle of fifths the vi–ii–V–I progression in the key of A Major. Name the chords involved and their nature.

Exercise 9.11: Draw on the circle of fifths the iii–vi–ii–V–I progression in the key of Db Major. Name the chords involved and their nature.

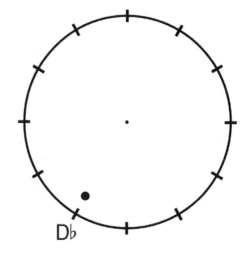

Exercise 9.12: Draw on the circle of fifths the iii–vi–ii–V–I progression in the key of E Major. Name the chords involved and their nature.

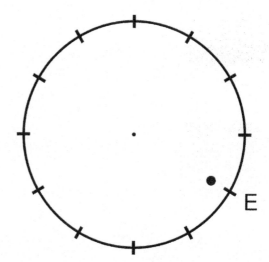

Notes

10 - Whole tone and other scales

The examples of the different scales follow the work in Chapter 10 of *The Circle of Fifths* and the exercises are numbered accordingly.

The whole tone scale

This is a six notes scale repeating at the octave. Composed of two interlocking augmented triads, there can only be two distinct sets of notes within the octave and these are usually designated as the C whole tone scale and the Db whole tone scale.

First a short note on why C and Db are usually the designated tonics. The Caug triad is C E G#. If we were to start with G# and build the augmented triad in an ascending fashion, as is usual practice in music theory, the G#aug triad would be G# B# D## in order to respect the principal of major thirds. To avoid double sharps or flats, we adopt the simplicity of using C and C# (or Db) as the two tonics.

All other variations starting on different notes are simply modes of these two.

Example 10.1: Draw on the circle, the E mode of the C whole tone scale.

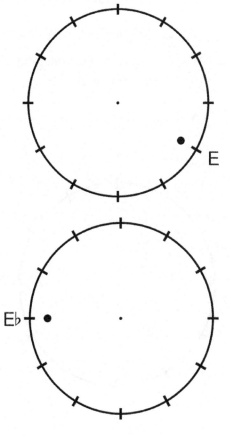

Example 10.2: Draw on the circle, the Eb mode of the Db whole tone scale.

The diminished scale

This eight note scale is closely connected with the diminished seventh chord which we have studied and practiced in Chapter 7. It is composed of alternating intervals of whole tones and semitones. Because of its symmetrical nature, there are only three discrete sets of notes which are conventionally named:

- C diminished
- C# diminished
- D diminished

All other collections are modes of these three.

There are two ways to visualize a tone/semitone diminished scale on the circle of fifths:

1. Probably the easiest to start with is to visualize on the circle:
   - ascending whole tone steps (two steps clockwise on the circle) like for the whole tone scale
   - ascending semitone steps (five steps anticlockwise on the circle)

2. To visualize it as formed from two diminished seventh chords formed:
   - on the first degree and
   - on the second degree, 1 tone up from the first degree.

We will introduce some exercises to familiarize you with both methods.

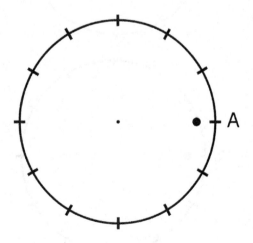

Example 10.3: Draw on the circle the notes of the A mode of the tone/semitone diminished scale. Identify the two component diminished seventh chords and to which member of the family of three diminished scales this mode belongs.

Example 10.4: Draw on the circle the notes of the D# mode of the tone/semitone diminished scale. Identify the two component diminished seventh chords and to which member of the family of three diminished scales this mode belongs.

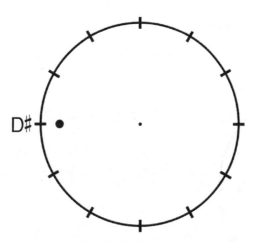

Example 10.5: Draw on the circle the notes of the Bb mode of the tone/semitone diminished scale. Identify the two component diminished seventh chords and to which member of the family of three diminished scales this mode belongs.

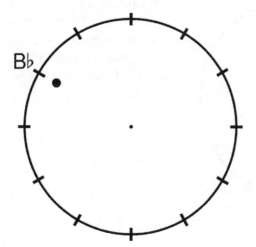

The inverted diminished scale

Called inverted because this version is built of semitones and whole tones, starting with a semitone. These scales are in fact modes of the whole tone/semitone scale.

Let's have a look at some examples.

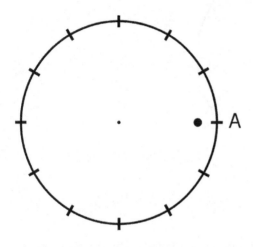

Example 10.6: Draw on the circle the notes of the A mode of the semitone/tone inverted diminished scale. Identify the two component diminished seventh chords and to which member of the family of three diminished scales this mode belongs.

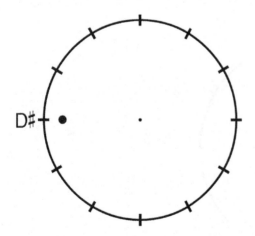

Example 10.7: Draw on the circle the notes of the D# mode of the semitone/tone inverted diminished scale. Identify the two component diminished seventh chords and to which member of the family of three diminished scales this mode belongs.

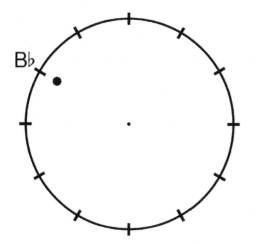

Example 10.8: Draw on the circle the notes of the Bb mode of the semitone/tone inverted diminished scale. Identify the two component diminished seventh chords and to which member of the family of three diminished scales this mode belongs.

Example 10.9: Compare the results of these pairs of examples:

- Examples 10.3 and 10.6
- Examples 10.4 and 10.7
- Examples 10.5 and 10.8

The diminished whole tone scale

It is not very useful to plot this scale on the circle other than to show that it does contain a pentatonic scale on its 5th degree. The pattern is not one that lends itself to rapid visualization.

The importance of this scale is largely related to improvising over altered dominants and perhaps the easiest way to conjure up this scale is to take the major scale on the same tonic and flatten all degrees except the tonic. This is also why it is known as the Superlocrian scale.

The pentatonic major and minor scales

The pentatonic major scale is a five note subset of our regular heptatonic major scale, using only the 1 2 3 5 6 degrees of the major scale. The minor pentatonic scale is the relative minor of the major pentatonic and is in fact the 5th mode of the major pentatonic scale.

As an example, C major pentatonic is C D E G A and its relative minor pentatonic is A C D E G, the fifth mode. That is, taking the the major pentatonic and starting to list the notes from the 5th note, A, and rotating them in the same order since the scale repeats at the octave.

If you wish to derive the minor pentatonic directly from the major scale with the same tonic note then you will apply the melodic formula: 1 b3 4 5 b7.

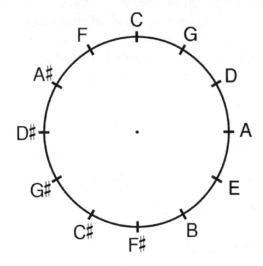

Example 10.10: Plot on the circle, the G major pentatonic scale, number the degrees and name the intervals between the scale degrees.

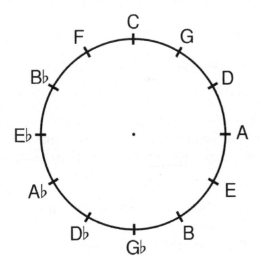

Example 10.11: Plot on the circle, the F major pentatonic scale, number the degrees and name the intervals between the scale degrees.

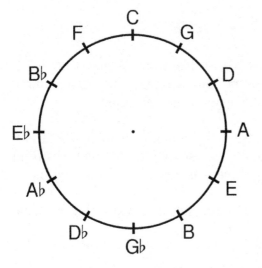

Example 10.12: Plot on the circle, the Ab major pentatonic scale, number the degrees and name the intervals between the scale degrees.

Example 10.13: Plot on the circle, the D minor pentatonic scale, number the degrees and name the intervals between the scale degrees.

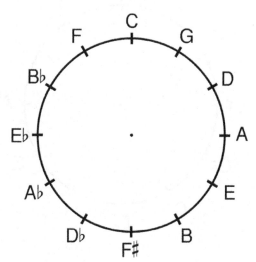

Example 10.14: Plot on the circle, the B minor pentatonic scale, number the degrees and name the intervals between the scale degrees.

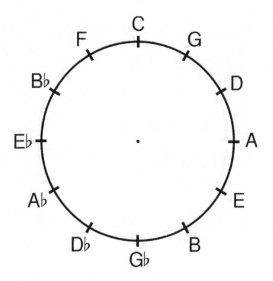

Example 10.15: Plot on the circle, the Bb minor pentatonic scale, number the degrees and name the intervals between the scale degrees.

Now for some examples for improvisers

When improvising, pentatonics can provide a different sound palette and you will have the artistic choice to make whether to stay in the key or to go outside. It is helpful to understand which pentatonic sets of notes are available to you which ever choice you make.

First, major key examples

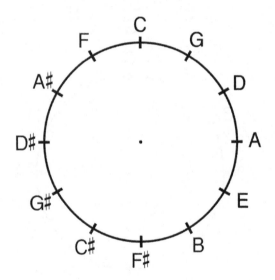

Example 10.16: Indicate on the circle the pentatonic scales which are 'inside' the key of A Major.

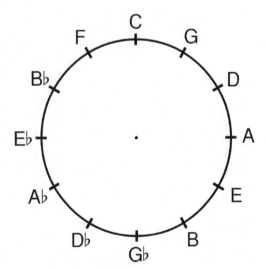

Example 10.17: Indicate on the circle the pentatonic scales which are 'inside' the key of Bb Major.

Example 10.18: Indicate on the circle the penta-tonic scales which are 'inside' the key of Db Major.

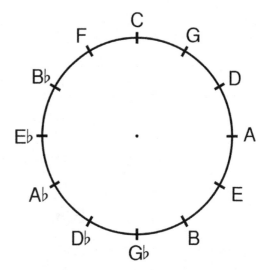

Some examples in minor keys

Minor harmony is made all the more rich because of the ability to pick and choose between the different flavors - harmonic, natural and melodic. Although there is no pentatonic scale entirely within the harmonic minor scale, there is one pentatonic set inside the ascending melodic scale which is also sometimes known as the jazz minor scale. Because the natural minor is a mode of the major scale using the same set of notes, it has the three possibilities of inside pentatonic scales.

Example 10.19: Indicate on the circle the penta-tonic scales inside the D melodic minor ascending scale.

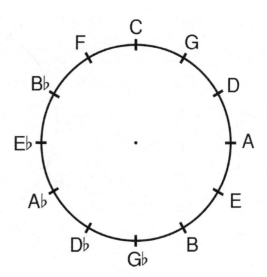

Example 10.20: Indicate on the circle the pentatonic scales inside the F melodic minor ascending scale.

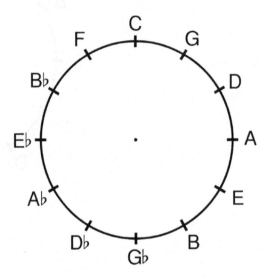

Example 10.21: Indicate on the circle the pentatonic scales inside the Eb melodic minor ascending scale.

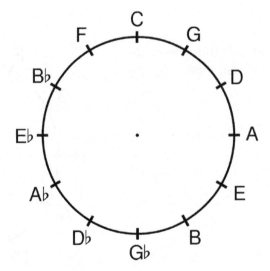

The Blues scale

The classic and traditional version of the Blues scale is a minor pentatonic scale with an additional note, the flattened fifth: 1 b3 4 b5 5 b7. It can be visualized on the circle as a minor pentatonic with the additional note formed as a tritone from the tonic, a simple task on the circle as we saw in Chapter 6.

Example 10.22: Indicate on the circle the Blues scale on F, number the degrees, name the intervals between the scale degrees and indicate its melodic description.

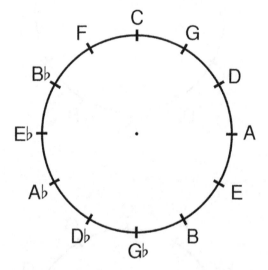

Example 10.23: Indicate on the circle the Blues scale on G, number the degrees, name the intervals between the scale degrees and indicate its melodic description.

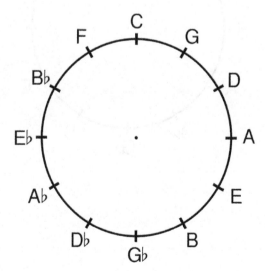

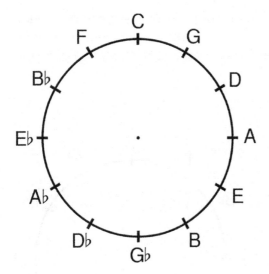

Example 10.24: Indicate on the circle the Blues scale on E, number the degrees, name the intervals between the scale degrees and indicate its melodic description.

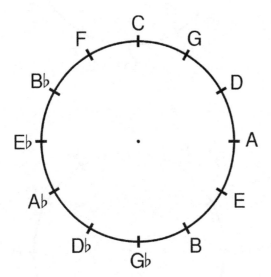

Example 10.25: Indicate on the circle the Blues scale on Eb, number the degrees, name the intervals between the scale degrees and indicate its melodic description.

11 - Chord Scales – Major Scale

In this chapter we present some exercises to help with deciding which scale is available for any given chord. Where did that chord come from?

The examples should be read in conjunction with Chapter 11 of the *The Circle of Fifths*.

We will look at the harmonization of the major scale. The harmonization of the minor scales will follow in Volume 3 of the workbook.

The major scale

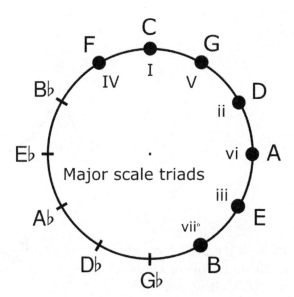

Major scale triads

We will look at examples for each of the chord types found in the harmonization of the major scale:

- major triads and tetrads
- dominant sevenths
- minor triads and tetrads
- the diminished triad
- half-diminished seventh

Example 11maj.1: You have a chord marked Db. In the harmonization of which major scales could this chord be found? Write the notes of the chord and indicate on the circle on which degrees this chord could be constructed.

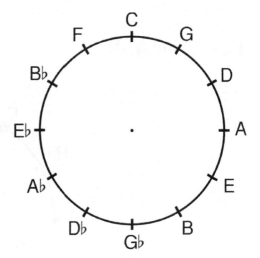

Example 11maj.2: You have a chord marked A. In the harmonization of which major scales could this chord be found? Write the notes of the chord and indicate on the circle on which degrees this chord could be constructed.

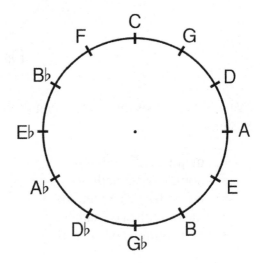

Example 11maj.3: You have a chord marked F. In the harmonization of which major scales could this chord be found? Write the notes of the chord and indicate on the circle on which degrees this chord could be constructed.

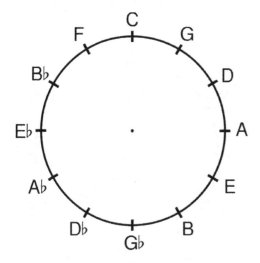

Example 11maj.4: You have a chord marked Emaj7. In the harmonization of which major scales could this chord be found? Write the notes of the chord and indicate on the circle on which degrees this chord could be constructed.

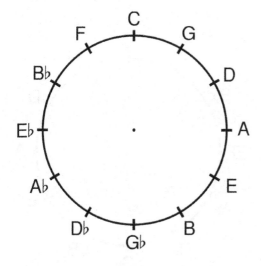

Example 11maj.5: You have a chord marked Ebmaj7. In the harmonization of which major scales could this chord be found? Write the notes of the chord and indicate on the circle on which degrees this chord could be constructed.

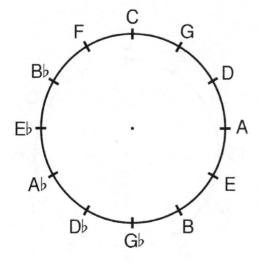

Example 11maj.6: You have a chord marked Dmaj7. In the harmonization of which major scales could this chord be found? Write the notes of the chord and indicate on the circle on which degrees this chord could be constructed.

Example 11maj.7: You have a chord marked D7. In the harmonization of which major scales could this chord be found? Write the notes of the chord and indicate on the circle on which degrees this chord could be constructed.

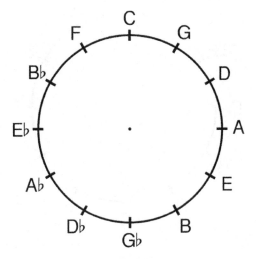

Example 11maj.8: You have a chord marked Ab7. In the harmonization of which major scales could this chord be found? Write the notes of the chord and indicate on the circle on which degrees this chord could be constructed.

Example 11maj.9: You have a chord marked Bb7. In the harmonization of which major scales could this chord be found? Write the notes of the chord and indicate on the circle on which degrees this chord could be constructed.

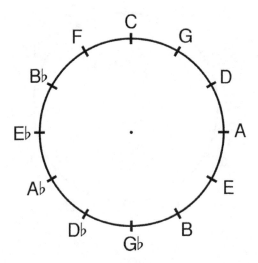

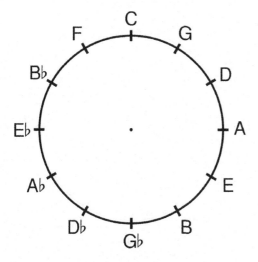

Example 11maj.10: You have a chord marked Gm7. In the harmonization of which major scales could this chord be found? Write the notes of the chord and indicate on the circle on which degrees this chord could be constructed.

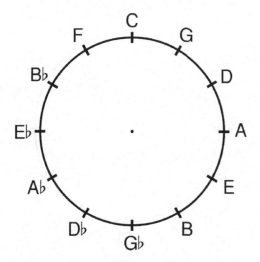

Example 11maj.11: You have a chord marked Ebm7. In the harmonization of which major scales could this chord be found? Write the notes of the chord and indicate on the circle on which degrees this chord could be constructed.

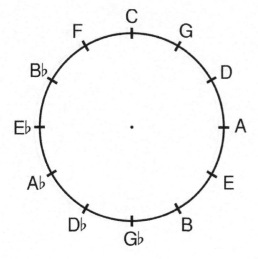

Example 11maj.12: You have a chord marked Em. In the harmonization of which major scales could this chord be found? Write the notes of the chord and indicate on the circle on which degrees this chord could be constructed.

Example 11maj.13: You have a chord marked Edim. In the harmonization of which major scales could this chord be found? Write the notes of the chord and indicate on the circle on which degrees this chord could be constructed.

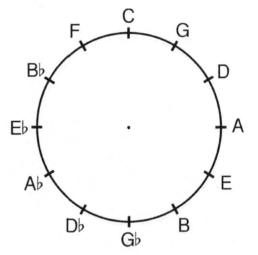

Example 11maj.14: You have a chord marked Gdim. In the harmonization of which major scales could this chord be found? Write the notes of the chord and indicate on the circle on which degrees this chord could be constructed.

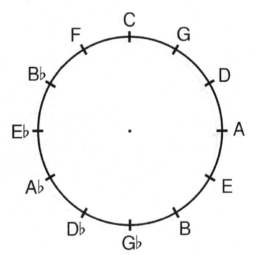

Example 11maj.15: You have a chord marked Am7b5. In the harmonization of which major scales could this chord be found? Write the notes of the chord and indicate on the circle on which degrees this chord could be constructed.

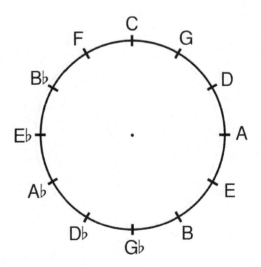

PART 2

Answers

Volume 2

Answers

In this second part of *The Workbook: Volume 2 – Further Steps,* we have included figures showing a correct answer to the examples given in each chapter of the first part of this workbook. Feedback from students has helped us to see where it is useful to provide some additional explanatory remarks.

The numbering of each chapter in Part 2 corresponds with the chapter numbering in Part 1 of this Workbook and also to the relevant chapter in *The Circle of Fifths.*

8: Substitute Dominants - Answers

Exercise 8.1: Draw the chromatic progression resulting from substituting the dominant 7th in a ii–V–I progression starting at Am7 and name the chords.

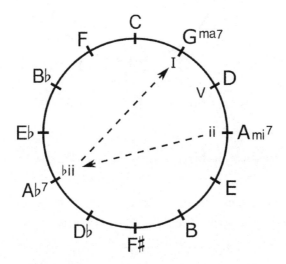

The original ii–V–I progression starting from Ami7 is Ami7–D7–Gma7.

The substitute dominant 7th for D7 is Ab7.

The new, chromatic progression ii–bii–I is Ami7–Ab7 – Gma7.

Exercise 8.2: Draw the chromatic progression resulting from substituting the dominant 7th in a ii–V–I progression starting at Emi7 and name the chords.

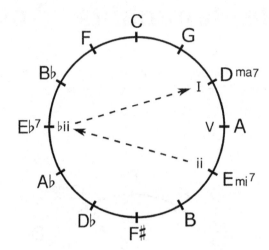

The original ii–V–I progression starting from Emi7 is Emi7–A7–Dma7.

The substitute dominant 7th for A7 is Eb7.

The new, chromatic progression ii–bii–I is Emi7–Eb7 – Dma7.

Exercise 8.3: Draw the chromatic progression resulting from substituting the dominant 7th in a ii–V–I progression starting at Bbmi7 and name the chords.

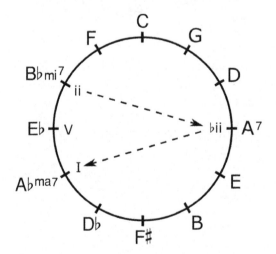

The original ii–V–I progression starting from Bbmi7 is Bbmi7–Eb7–Abma7.

The substitute dominant 7th for Eb7 is A7.

The new, chromatic progression ii–bii–I is Bbmi7–A7 – Abma7.

Exercise 8.4: Draw the chromatic progression resulting from substituting the dominant 7th in a ii–V–I progression starting at Fmi7 and name the chords.

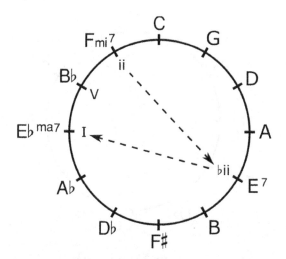

The original ii–V–I progression starting from Fmi7 is Fmi7–Bb7–Ebma7.

The substitute dominant 7th for Bb7 is E7.

The new, chromatic progression ii–bii–I is Fmi7–E7 – Ebma7.

Exercise 8.5: Draw the chromatic progression resulting from substituting the dominant 7th in a ii–V–I progression starting at F#mi7 and name the chords.

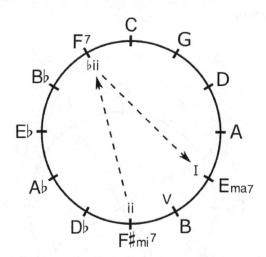

The original ii–V–I progression starting from F#mi7 is F#mi7–B7–Ema7.

The substitute dominant 7th for B7 is F7.

The new, chromatic progression ii–bii–I is F#mi7–F7 – Ema7.

Exercise 8.6: Draw the chromatic progression resulting from substituting the dominant 7th in a ii–V–I progression starting at Abmi7 and name the chords.

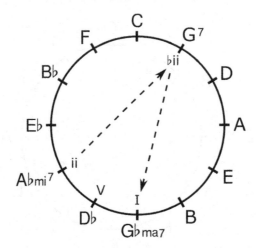

The original ii–V–I progression starting from Abmi7 is Abmi7–Db7–Gbma7.

The substitute dominant 7th for Db7 is G7.

The new, chromatic progression ii–bii–I is Abmi7–G7 – Gbma7.

Bartok Substitutions

Exercise 8.7: Mark the Bartok dominants and label their degrees for A Major tonality.

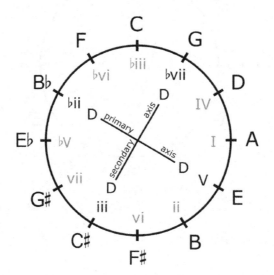

For A Major tonality, the Bartok dominants are:

1. Principal axis

    • E, degree V, the dominant of the A Major scale

    • Bb, degree bii

2. Secondary axis

    • C#, degree iii

    • G, degree bvii

Exercise 8.8: Mark the Bartok dominants and label their degrees for F Major tonality.

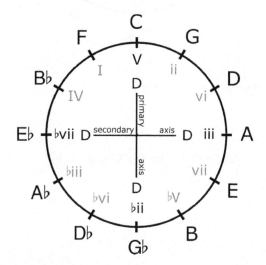

For F Major tonality, the Bartok dominants are:

1. Principal axis

    • C, degree V, the dominant of the F Major scale

    • Gb, degree bii

2. Secondary axis

    • A, degree iii

    • Eb, degree bvii

Exercise 8.9: Mark the Bartok dominants and label their degrees for Eb Major tonality.

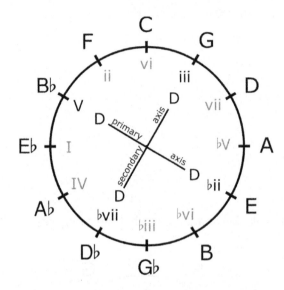

For Eb Major tonality, the Bartok dominants are:

1. Principal axis

    *   Bb, degree V, the dominant of the Eb Major scale

    *   E, degree bii

2. Secondary axis

    *   G, degree iii

    *   Db, degree bvii

Note: in this example, I have purposely ignored a part of the naming conventions required by strict application of musical theory.

In Eb Major, the bii would be Fb which I have left as E. Similarly, bvi is Cb which I have left at B. There comes a time when you may prefer to choose the practical approach and this is even more true when the strictly correct approach would mean using double flats or double sharps. For example, the bV could be written as Bbb which in more practical terms is the same sound as A.

Exercise 8.10: Mark the Bartok dominants and label their degrees for Db Major tonality.

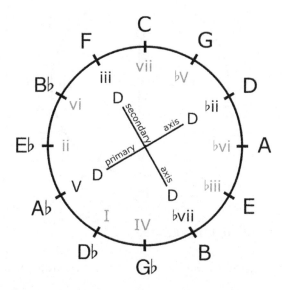

For Db Major tonality, the Bartok dominants are:

1. Principal axis

   • Ab, degree V, the dominant of the Db Major scale

   • D, degree bii

2. Secondary axis

   • F, degree iii

   • B, degree bvii

Exercise 8.11: Mark the Bartok dominants and label their degrees for B Major tonality.

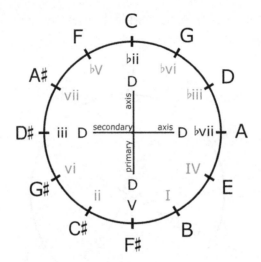

For B Major tonality, the Bartok dominants are:

1. Principal axis : F#, degree V, the dominant of the B Major scale; C, degree bii

2. Secondary axis: D#, degree iii; A, degree bvii

Exercise 8.12: Mark the Bartok dominants and label their degrees for D Major tonality.

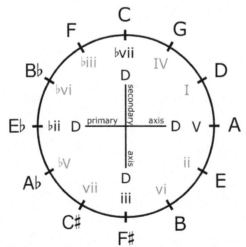

For D Major tonality, the Bartok dominants are:

1. Principal axis: A, degree V, the dominant of the D Major scale; Eb, degree bii

2. Secondary axis: F#, degree iii; C, degree bvii

9: Chord Progressions - Answers

Don't forget that blank sheets with circles are available as a free download to help you in your work. See the 'Resources' section of this book for the download link.

The 2 5 1 progression

Exercise 9.1: Draw on the circle of fifths the ii–V–I progression in the key of D Major. Name the chords involved and their nature.

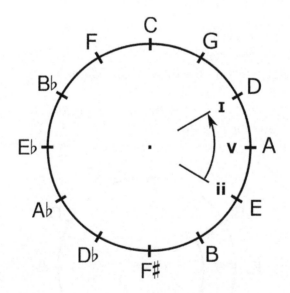

The chords involved in a ii–V–I progression in D Major are:

- ii is Em7   minor seventh

- V is A7   dominant seventh

- I is Dmaj7   major seventh - the tonic of D Major key.

Exercise 9.2: Draw on the circle of fifths the ii–V–I progression in the key of Bb Major. Name the chords involved and their nature.

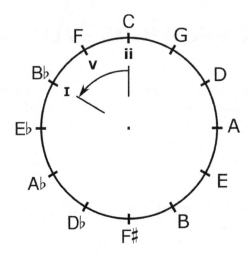

The chords involved in a ii–V–I progression in Bb Major are:

- ii is Cm7   minor seventh
- V is F7   dominant seventh
- I is Bbmaj7   major seventh - the tonic of Bb Major key.

Exercise 9.3: Draw on the circle of fifths the ii–V–I progression in the key of Ab Major. Name the chords involved and their nature.

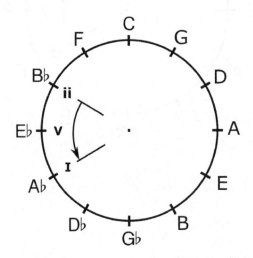

The chords involved in a ii–V–I progression in Ab Major are:

- ii is Bbm7   minor seventh
- V is Eb7   dominant seventh
- I is Abmaj7   major seventh - the tonic of Ab Major key.

Exercise 9.4: Draw on the circle of fifths the ii–V–I progression in the key of G Major. Name the chords involved and their nature.

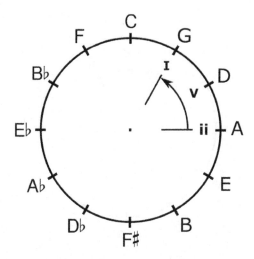

The chords involved in a ii–V–I progression in G Major are:

- ii is Am7   minor seventh
- V is D7   dominant seventh
- I is Gmaj7   major seventh - the tonic of G Major key.

Exercise 9.5: Draw on the circle of fifths the ii–V–I progression in the key of F# Major. Name the chords involved and their nature.

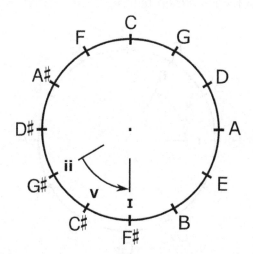

The chords involved in a ii–V–I progression in F# Major are:

- ii is G#m7   minor seventh
- V is C#7   dominant seventh
- I is F#maj7   major seventh - the tonic of F# Major key.

Exercise 9.6: Draw on the circle of fifths the ii–V–I progression in the key of F harmonic minor. Name the chords involved and their nature.

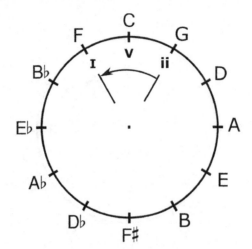

The chords involved in a ii–V–I progression in harmonic minor have a different nature when compared with a major key and for F harmonic minor are:

- ii is Gm7b5   half diminished, that is a minor seventh with b5
- V is C7b9   dominant seventh with a b9
- I is Fm.maj7   F minor with a major seventh - the tonic of F harmonic minor key.

Exercise 9.7: Draw on the circle of fifths the ii–V–I progression in the key of Eb harmonic minor. Name the chords involved and their nature.

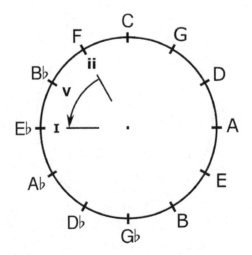

The chords involved in a ii–V–I progression in Eb harmonic minor are:

- ii is Fm7b5   half diminished, that is a minor seventh with b5
- V is Bb7b9   dominant seventh with a b9
- I is Ebm.maj7   Eb minor with major seventh - the tonic of Eb harmonic minor key.

Exercise 9.8: Draw on the circle of fifths the ii–V–I progression in the key of B harmonic minor. Name the chords involved and their nature.

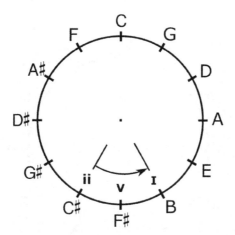

The chords involved in a ii–V–I progression in B harmonic minor are:

- ii is C#m7b5   half diminished, that is a minor seventh with b5
- V is F#7b9   dominant seventh with a b9
- I is Bm.maj7   B minor with a major seventh - the tonic of B harmonic minor key.

Other progressions

Exercise 9.9: Draw on the circle of fifths the vi–ii–V–I progression in the key of Bb Major. Name the chords involved and their nature.

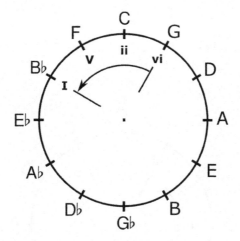

The chords involved in a vi–ii–V–I progression in Bb Major are:

- vi is Gm7   minor seventh
- ii is Cm7   minor seventh
- V is F7   dominant seventh
- I is Bbmaj7   Bb major seventh - the tonic of Bb Major key.

Exercise 9.10: Draw on the circle of fifths the vi–ii–V–I progression in the key of A Major. Name the chords involved and their nature.

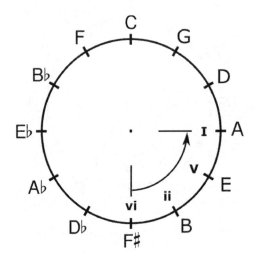

The chords involved in a vi–ii–V–I progression in A Major are:

- vi is F#m7   minor seventh
- ii is Bm7   minor seventh
- V is E7   dominant seventh
- I is Amaj7   A major seventh - the tonic of A Major key.

Exercise 9.11: Draw on the circle of fifths the iii–vi–ii–V–I progression in the key of Db Major. Name the chords involved and their nature.

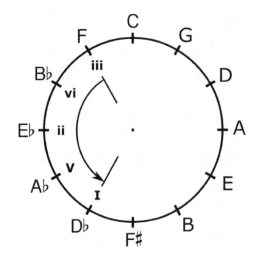

The chords involved in a iii–vi–ii–V–I progression in Db Major are:

- iii is Fm7   minor seventh
- vi is Bbm7   minor seventh
- ii is Ebm7   minor seventh
- V is Ab7   dominant seventh
- I is Dbmaj7   Db major seventh - the tonic of Db Major key.

Exercise 9.12: Draw on the circle of fifths the iii–vi–ii–V–I progression in the key of E Major. Name the chords involved and their nature.

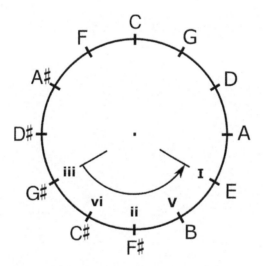

The chords involved in a iii–vi–ii–V–I progression in E Major are:

- iii is G#m7   minor seventh
- vi is C#m7   minor seventh
- ii is F#m7   minor seventh
- V is B7   dominant seventh
- I is Emaj7   E major seventh - the tonic of E Major key.

Notes

10: Whole tone and other scales - Answers

Example 10.1: Draw on the circle, the E mode of the C whole tone scale.

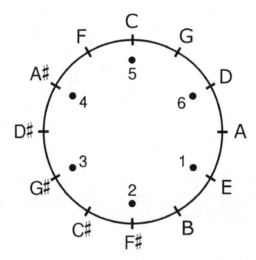

The key to this plot is visualizing ascending whole tones or steps, major seconds, on the circle. Starting at E, take two steps round clockwise to F# and continue to complete the E mode of C whole tone scale: E F# G# A# C D.

Note that this is the practical answer to use C instead of B# and D instead of C##. Always take the practical solution unless you're involved in a theory exam where strict adherence to theory is required.

Example 10.2: Draw on the circle, the Eb mode of the Db whole tone scale.

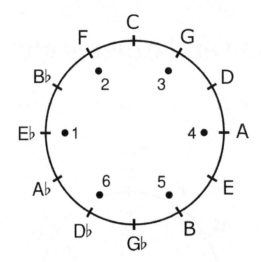

The notes of the Eb mode of the Db (C#) whole tone scale are: Eb F G A B Db

Example 10.3: Draw on the circle the notes of the A mode of the tone/semitone diminished scale. Identify the two component diminished seventh chords and to which member of the family of three diminished scales this mode belongs.

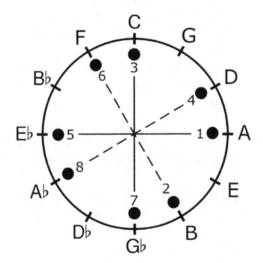

Follow the numbers to see the sequence of plotting by successive whole tones (t) and semi-tones (s):

A (t) B (s) C (t) D (s) Eb (t) F (s) Gb (t) Ab (s) A

Note that this movement is a sequence of "2 steps clockwise" (up a whole tone or a whole step) followed by "5 steps anticlockwise" (up a semitone or a half-step).

This is made of two diminished seventh chords :

- the odd degrees   1,3,5,7 A C Eb Gb,   shown with solid lines
- the even degrees   2,4,6,8 B D F Ab,   shown with dashed lines

If it helps, you can think of these two dim7 chords as being on the first and second degrees of the diminished scale (mode). That is on A and B.

Or think in terms of the major scale on the same tonic and build the two dim7 chords on the tonic and IV degree of this major scale. You will remember from Chapter 2 that the degree IV is one step round anticlockwise from the tonic. In this case, on A and D.

For tone/semitone diminished scales, this amounts to the same thing BUT NOT for the inverted diminished scale with semitone/tone intervals.

In this example, the A diminished scale is a mode of the C diminished (t-s) scale.

Example 10.4: Draw on the circle the notes of the D# mode of the tone/semitone diminished scale. Identify the two component diminished seventh chords and to which member of the family of three diminished scales this mode belongs.

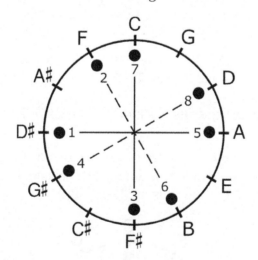

Follow the numbers to see the sequence of plotting by successive whole tones (t) and semitones (s):   D# (t) F (s) F# (t) G# (s) A (t) B (s) C (t) D (s) D#

This is basically the same case as in Ex 10.3 above but with enharmonic spelling. The two dim7 chords are the same :

- the odd degrees   1,3,5,7 D# F# A C   shown with solid lines
- the even degrees   2,4,6,8 F G# B D   shown with dashed lines

In this example, the D# diminished scale is a mode of the C diminished (t-s) scale.

Example 10.5: Draw on the circle the notes of the Bb mode of the tone/semitone diminished scale. Identify the two component diminished seventh chords and to which member of the family of three diminished scales this mode belongs.

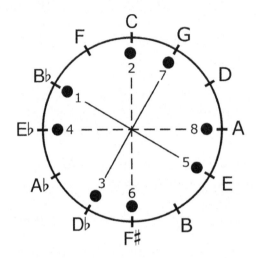

Follow the numbers to see the sequence of plotting by successive whole tones (t) and semi-tones (s):   Bb (t) C (s) Db (t) Eb (s) E (t) F# (s) G (t) A (s) Bb

The two dim7 chords are :

•	the odd degrees	1,3,5,7 Bb Db E G	shown with solid lines
•	the even degrees	2,4,6,8 C Eb F# A	shown with dashed lines

In this example, the Bb diminished scale is a mode of the C# or Db diminished (t-s) scale.

Example 10.6: Draw on the circle the notes of the A mode of the semitone/tone inverted diminished scale. Identify the two component diminished seventh chords and to which member of the family of three diminished scales this mode belongs.

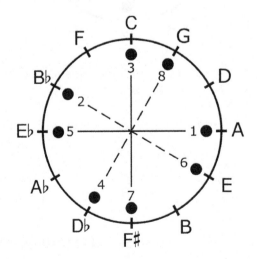

Follow the numbers to see the sequence of plotting by successive semitones (s) and whole tones (t):

A (s) Bb (t) C (s) Db (t) Eb (s) E (t) F# (s) G (t) A

This is made of two diminished seventh chords :

- the odd degrees   1,3,5,7 A C Eb Gb (F#)   shown with solid lines
- the even degrees   2,4,6,8 Bb Db E G   shown with dashed lines

In this example, the A inverted diminished (s-t) scale is a mode of the C# diminished (t-s) scale.

Example 10.7: Draw on the circle the notes of the D# mode of the semitone/tone inverted diminished scale. Identify the two component diminished seventh chords and to which member of the family of three diminished scales this mode belongs.

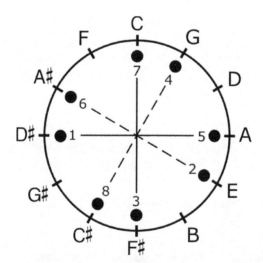

Follow the numbers to see the sequence of plotting by successive semitones (s) and whole tones (t):

D# (s) E (t) F# (s) G (t) A (s) A# (t) C (s) C# (t) D#

This is made of two diminished seventh chords :

- the odd degrees   1,3,5,7 D# F# A C   shown with solid lines
- the even degrees   2,4,6,8 E G A# C#   shown with dashed lines

In this example, the D# inverted diminished (s-t) scale is a mode of the C# diminished (t-s) scale.

Example 10.8: Draw on the circle the notes of the Bb mode of the semitone/tone inverted diminished scale. Identify the two component diminished seventh chords and to which member of the family of three diminished scales this mode belongs.

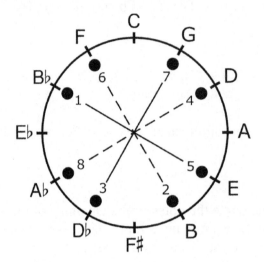

Follow the numbers to see the sequence of plotting by successive semitones (s) and whole tones (t):

Bb (s) B (t) Db (s) D (t) E (s) F (t) G (s) Ab...(t)...Bb

The two dim7 chords are :

- the odd degrees 1,3,5,7 Bb Db E G shown with solid lines
- the even degrees 2,4,6,8 B D F Ab shown with dashed lines

In this example, the Bb inverted diminished (s-t) scale is a mode of the D diminished (t-s) scale.

Example 10.9: Compare the results of these pairs of examples:

- Examples 10.3 and 10.6

- Examples 10.4 and 10.7

- Examples 10.5 and 10.8

Look at the composite image below showing the results of Examples 10.3 and 10.6 :

On the left you see the typical tone / semitone diminished scale and on the right the typical inverse diminished scale, semitone / tone, both with tonic A. Note how the two dim7 chords are placed in each version.

Example 10.3   Example 10.6

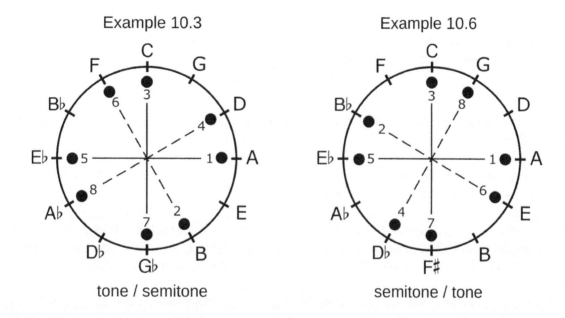

tone / semitone   semitone / tone

So much in music theory is related back to a major scale. So, now let us relate these two versions of a diminished scale to a major scale having the same tonic, A. You will recall from Chapter 2, that on the circle of fifths, the three principal degrees of the major scale, I, IV and V, are grouped together. Degree V is one step round clockwise from the tonic and degree IV is one step anticlockwise. Now look at the more generic illustration below.

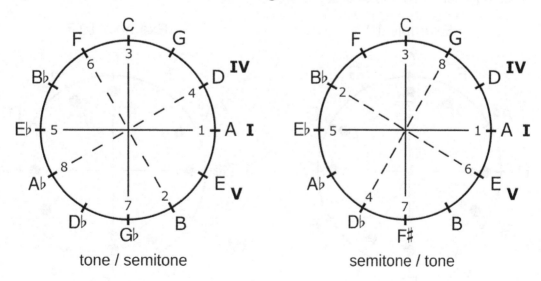

tone / semitone   semitone / tone

What we can learn from this example is that to form a tone / semitone diminished scale on any given tonic note, we can visualize the major scale on the same tonic and use the notes from two dim7 chords:

1. constructed on the tonic
2. constructed on the IV degree of the major scale

Similarly, to form a semitone / tone inverted diminished scale on any given tonic note, we can take the major scale on the same tonic and use the notes from two dim7 chords:

1. constructed on the tonic
2. constructed on the V degree of the major scale

This is first of all consistent with musical practice in using the major scale as a starting point and secondly, simple to visualize on the circle because we have seen in Chapter 2 that degrees IV, I, V are adjacent notes on the circle with IV and V being on either side of the tonic.

As practical musicians, we are not necessarily so much interested in the scale order of the notes but rather which are the notes forming the set we want to use. In improvisation, we are generally rather unlikely to play the full set of notes in scale order.

For completeness, I have included the comparisons of the other two example sets where you can confirm the findings.

First the comparison of Examples 10.4 and 10.7 :

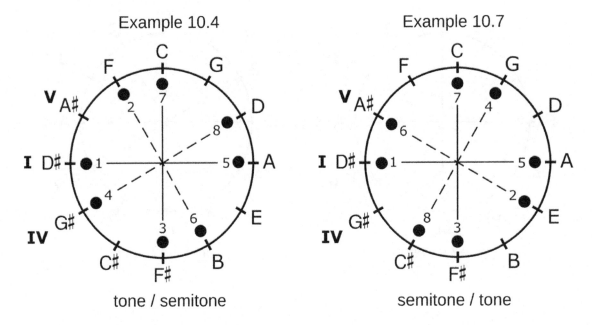

Here you see that to form a tone / semitone diminished scale on D#, use the notes of two diminished seventh chords – one formed on the tonic D# and the other on the IV degree of D# Major, G#, one step round the circle anticlockwise.

Similarly, on the right hand side you see that the semitone / tone inverted diminished scale is formed of two diminished seventh chords on the tonic, D# and the V degree of D# Major, A#, one step clockwise round the circle.

And finally the comparison of Examples 10.5 and 10.8 :

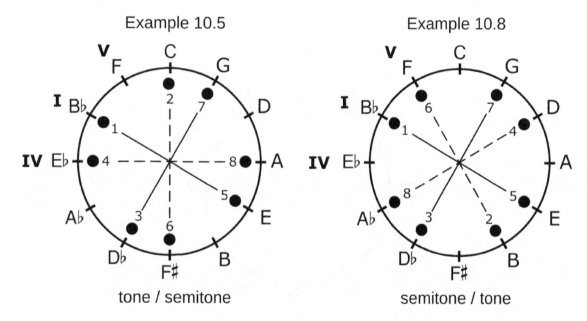

To form a tone semitone diminished scale on Bb, visualize two diminished seventh chords:

1. on Bb

2. the other on the IV degree of Bb Major, one step anticlockwise round the circle, Eb.

To form a semitone / tone inverted diminished scale on Bb, visualize two diminished seventh chords:

1. on Bb

2. the other on the V degree of Bb Major, one step clockwise round the circle, F.

Pentatonic scales

First, some examples of the major pentatonic.

The rapid visualization technique to get the major pentatonic scale is to take 5 consecutive fifths up, that is clockwise, starting with the given tonic. This gives you the set of notes but not in scale order. Often, for playing, this is sufficient. In the examples below, we put the notes into scale order and indicate the intervals involved.

Example 10.10: Plot on the circle, the G major pentatonic scale, number the degrees and name the intervals between the scale degrees.

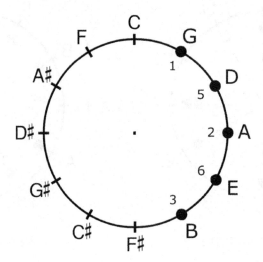

G D A E B is the set of notes we need. In scale order, you get the G major pentatonic scale which is: G A B D E labeled 1 2 3 5 6 by reference to the G Major scale.

For the intervals:

- G, the tonic, go up a major second, 2 steps clockwise, to

- A. Then up a major second to

- B. Then up a minor 3rd, 3 steps anticlockwise, to

- D. Then up a major second to

- E. Then up a minor 3rd to

- G, to start the next octave.

Example 10.11: Plot on the circle, the F major pentatonic scale, number the degrees and name the intervals between the scale degrees.

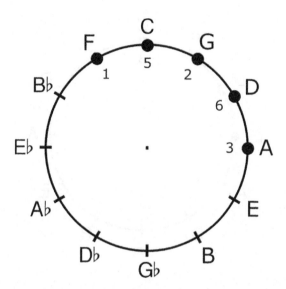

F C G D A is the set of notes we need. In scale order, you get the F major pentatonic scale: F G A C D labeled 1 2 3 5 6 by reference to the F Major scale with the same tonic.

For the intervals:

- F, the tonic, go up a major second, 2 steps clockwise, to

- G. Then up a major second to

- A. Then up a minor 3rd, 3 steps anticlockwise, to

- C. Then up a major second to

- D. Then up a minor 3rd to

- F, to start the next octave.

Example 10.12: Plot on the circle, the Ab major pentatonic scale, number the degrees and name the intervals between the scale degrees.

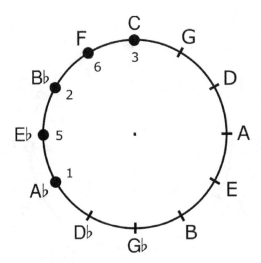

Ab Eb Bb F C is the set of notes we need. In scale order, you get the Ab major pentatonic scale: Ab Bb C Eb F labeled 1 2 3 5 6 by reference to the Ab Major scale.

For the intervals:

- Ab, the tonic, go up a major second, 2 steps clockwise, to

- Bb. Then up a major second to

- C. Then up a minor 3rd, 3 steps anticlockwise, to

- Eb. Then up a major second to

- F. Then up a minor 3rd to

- Ab, to start the next octave.

Now, for some examples of the minor pentatonic

The rapid visualization technique to get the minor pentatonic scale is again to take 5 consecutive fifths but this time we start with the given tonic, take the next one up, that is clockwise, and then take three more down, anticlockwise, from the tonic. This gives you the set of notes but not in scale order. This is usually sufficient. In the examples below, we put the notes into scale order and indicate the intervals involved.

Example 10.13: Plot on the circle, the D minor pentatonic scale, number the degrees and name the intervals between the scale degrees.

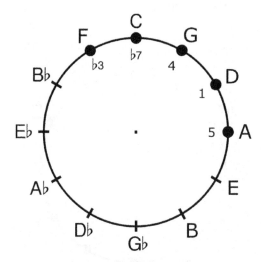

In this example, we take first the tonic, D, and then the next fifth upwards, A, plus the three down from D (F, C and G). Our set of notes for the D minor pentatonic is F C G D A and in scale order this becomes D F G A C labeled 1 b3 4 5 b7 by reference to the D Major scale.

You could arrive at the same result by reasoning as follows:

- I need D minor pentatonic

- its relative major will be F major pentatonic (refer to Chapter 5 *The Circle of Fifths*)

- therefore I start with F and take the next four steps upwards (clockwise)

The intervals involved in the D minor pentatonic scale are:

- D, the tonic, go up a minor 3rd to

- F. Then up a major second to

- G. Then up a major second to

- A. Then up a minor 3rd to

- C. Then up a major second to

- D, to start the next octave.

Example 10.14: Plot on the circle, the B minor pentatonic scale, number the degrees and name the intervals between the scale degrees.

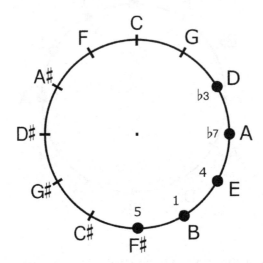

Our set of notes for the B minor pentatonic is D A E B F# and in scale order this becomes B D E F# A labeled 1 b3 4 5 b7 by reference to the B Major scale.

You could arrive at the same result by reasoning as follows:

• I need B minor pentatonic

• its relative major will be D major pentatonic (refer to Chapter 5 *The Circle of Fifths*)

• therefore I start with D and take the next four steps upwards (clockwise)

The intervals involved in the B minor pentatonic scale are:

• B, the tonic, go up a minor 3rd to

• D. Then up a major second to

• E. Then up a major second to

• F#. Then up a minor 3rd to

• A. Then up a major second to

• B, to start the next octave.

Example 10.15: Plot on the circle, the Bb minor pentatonic scale, number the degrees and name the intervals between the scale degrees.

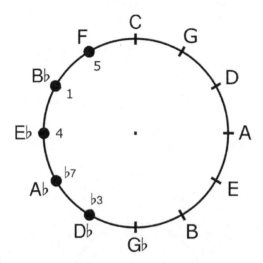

Our set of notes for the Bb minor pentatonic is Db Ab Eb Bb F and in scale order this becomes Bb Db Eb F Ab labeled 1 b3 4 5 b7 by reference to the Bb Major scale.

You could arrive at the same result by reasoning as follows:

- I need Bb minor pentatonic

- its relative major will be Db major pentatonic (refer to Chapter 5 *The Circle of Fifths*)

- therefore I start with Db and take the next four steps upwards (clockwise)

The intervals involved in the Bb minor pentatonic scale are:

- Bb, the tonic, go up a minor 3rd to

- Db. Then up a major second to

- Eb. Then up a major second to

- F. Then up a minor 3rd to

- Ab. Then up a major second to

- Bb, to start the next octave.

Next, the examples for improvisers

We'll look more closely at pentatonic scales that are inside a given tonality, major or minor. Of course, when improvising you will be free to play inside or outside the key. This is your artistic choice.

Major tonalities

Example 10.16: Indicate on the circle the pentatonic scales which are 'inside' the key of A Major.

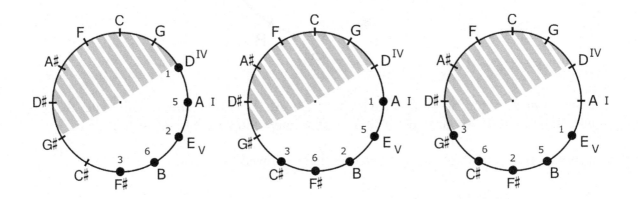

The image above shows the A Major scale notes in the clear half of the circles: A B C# D E F# G#. The three principal degrees of the scale are labeled: the tonic, A I; the sub-dominant, D IV; the dominant, E V.

It should be clear that a pentatonic scale of five successive fifths can be constructed on each of these principal degrees of the major scale and only on these three degrees.

Therefore, there are three pentatonic scales which are perfectly 'inside' the key of A Major and these are, from left to right:

- D major pentatonic: D E F# A B, on the sub-dominant, D

- A major pentatonic: A B C# E F#, on the tonic, A

- E major pentatonic: E F# G# B C#, on the dominant, E

Example 10.17: Indicate on the circle the pentatonic scales which are 'inside' the key of Bb Major.

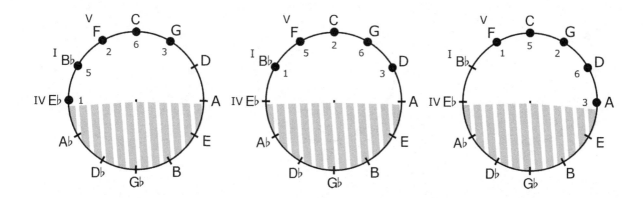

The image above shows the Bb Major scale notes in the clear half of the circles: Bb C D Eb F G. The three principal degrees of the scale are labeled: the tonic, Bb I; the sub-dominant, Eb IV; the dominant, F V.

It should by now be clear that a pentatonic scale of five successive fifths can be constructed on each of these principal degrees of the major scale and only on these three degrees.

Therefore, there are three pentatonic scales which are perfectly 'inside' the key of Bb Major and these are, from left to right:

- Eb major pentatonic: Eb F G Bb C, on the sub-dominant, Eb

- Bb major pentatonic: Bb C D F G, on the tonic, Bb

- F major pentatonic: F G A C D, on the dominant, F

Example 10.18: Indicate on the circle the pentatonic scales which are 'inside' the key of Db Major.

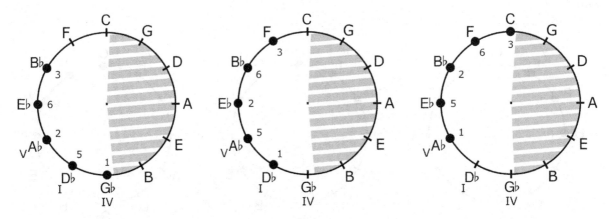

The image above shows the Db Major scale notes in the clear half of the circles: Db Eb F Gb Ab Bb C. The three principal degrees of the scale are labeled: the tonic, Db I; the sub-dominant, Gb IV; the dominant, Ab V.

It is now, I hope, clear that a pentatonic scale of five successive fifths can be constructed on each of these principal degrees of the major scale and only on these three degrees.

Therefore, there are three pentatonic scales which are perfectly 'inside' the key of Db Major and these are, from left to right:

- Gb major pentatonic: Gb Ab Bb Db Eb, on the sub-dominant, Gb

- Db major pentatonic: Db Eb F Ab Bb, on the tonic, Db

- Ab major pentatonic: Ab Bb C Eb F, on the dominant, Ab

Minor tonalities

Example 10.19: Indicate on the circle the pentatonic scales inside the D melodic minor ascending scale.

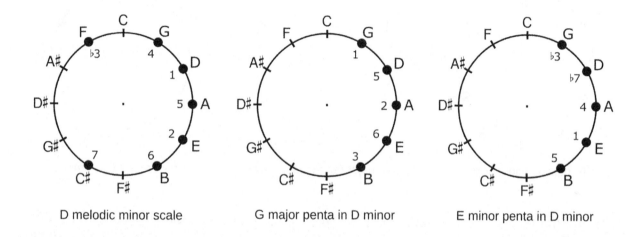

D melodic minor scale   G major penta in D minor   E minor penta in D minor

The illustration above shows, on the left, the notes of the D melodic minor ascending scale: D E F G A B C#. Note that in this minor scale, only the 3rd degree is flattened; F instead of F#. The 6th and 7th degrees are as in the D Major scale.

The central part of the illustration shows the only set of five consecutive notes on the circle which can form a pentatonic scale: G D A E B. In this central part of the figure, these five notes are labeled as G major pentatonic.

The right hand part of the figure shows this same set of five notes labeled as E minor pentatonic.

You will note that this single set of five notes within the melodic minor scale can be expressed as

- either G major pentatonic

- or E minor pentatonic

- E minor being the relative minor of G Major (recall the exercises of the relatives in chapter 5 of *The Circle of Fifths*)

Example 10.20: Indicate on the circle the pentatonic scales inside the F melodic minor ascending scale.

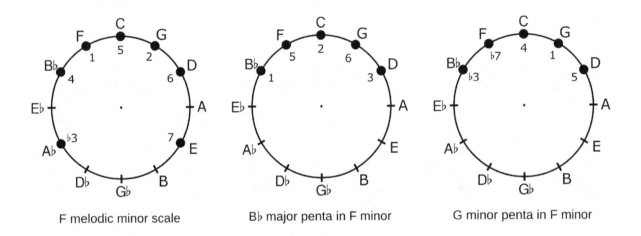

F melodic minor scale   Bb major penta in F minor   G minor penta in F minor

The illustration above shows on the left the notes of the F melodic minor ascending scale: F G Ab Bb C D E. Note that in this minor scale, only the 3rd degree is flattened; Ab instead of A. The 6th and 7th degrees are as in the F Major scale.

The central part of the illustration shows the only set of five consecutive notes on the circle which can form a pentatonic scale: Bb F C G D. In this central part of the figure, these five notes are labeled as Bb major pentatonic.

The right hand part of the figure shows this same set of five notes labeled as G minor pentatonic.

You will notes that this single set of five notes within the melodic minor scale can be expressed as

- either Bb major pentatonic

- or G minor pentatonic

- G minor being the relative minor of Bb Major (recall the exercises of the relatives in chapter 5 of *The Circle of Fifths*)

Example 10.21: Indicate on the circle the pentatonic scales inside the Eb melodic minor ascending scale.

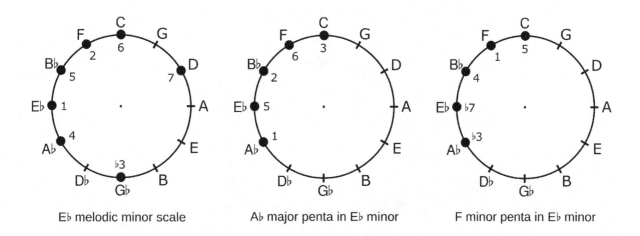

Eb melodic minor scale   Ab major penta in Eb minor   F minor penta in Eb minor

The illustration above shows on the left the notes of the Eb melodic minor ascending scale: Eb F Gb Ab Bb C D. Note that in this minor scale, only the 3rd degree is flattened; Gb instead of G. The 6th and 7th degrees are as in the Eb Major scale.

The central part of the illustration shows the only set of five consecutive notes on the circle which can form a pentatonic scale: Ab Eb Bb F C. In this central part of the figure, these five notes are labeled as Ab major pentatonic.

The right hand part of the figure shows this same set of five notes labeled as F minor pentatonic.

You will notes that this single set of five notes within the melodic minor scale can be expressed as

- either Ab major pentatonic

- or F minor pentatonic

- F minor being the relative minor of Ab Major (recall the exercises of the relatives in chapter 5 of *The Circle of Fifths*)

The Blues scale

Example 10.22: Indicate on the circle the Blues scale on F, number the degrees, name the intervals between the scale degrees and indicate its melodic description.

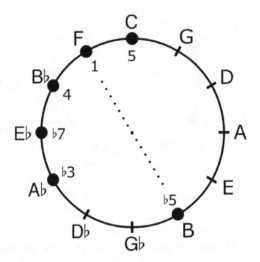

First plot the minor pentatonic scale as described in Example 10.13 above — first the tonic, F, and then the next fifth upwards, C, plus the three down from F (Ab Eb and Bb). Then add the note a tritone up from the tonic, B. This gives us the set of notes: Ab, Eb, Bb, F, C, B enharmonic respelling of Cb. This, in the ascending order gives the Blues scale in F:

F Ab Bb B C Eb with melodic analysis: 1 b3 4 b5 5 b7

by reference to the major scale with the same tonic, F Major. Note that the blue note, b5, is alternatively named #4 which amounts to the same thing.

The intervals involved in the F Blues scale are:

- F, the tonic, go up a minor 3rd to

- Ab. Then up a major second to

- Bb. Then up a semitone to

- B. Then up a semitone to

- C. Then up a minor 3rd to

- Eb. Then up a major second to

- F, to start the next octave.

Follow the movement round the circle as you read these intervals.

Example 10.23: Indicate on the circle the Blues scale on G, number the degrees, name the intervals between the scale degrees and indicate its melodic description.

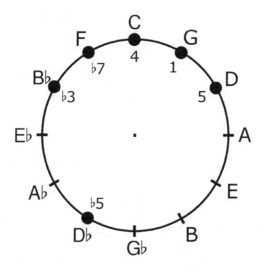

Our set of notes for G Blues is Bb, F, C, G, D, Db and in scale order this becomes G Bb C Db D F labeled 1 b3 4 b5 5 b7 by reference to the G Major scale.

The intervals involved in the G Blues scale are:

- G, the tonic, go up a minor 3rd to

- Bb. Then up a major second to

- C. Then up a semitone to

- Db. Then up a semitone to

- D. Then up a minor 3rd to

- F. Then up a major second to

- G, to start the next octave.

To help your visual memory, follow the movements round the circle as you read the intervals listed above.

Example 10.24: Indicate on the circle the Blues scale on E, number the degrees, name the intervals between the scale degrees and indicate its melodic description.

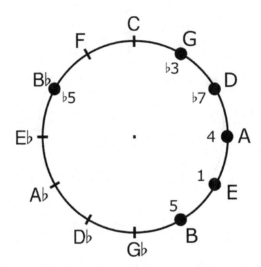

Our set of notes for E Blues is G, D, A, E, B, Bb and in scale order this becomes E G A Bb B D labeled 1 b3 4 b5 5 b7 by reference to the E Major scale.

The intervals involved in the E Blues scale are:

- E, the tonic, go up a minor 3rd to

- G. Then up a major second to

- A. Then up a semitone to

- Bb. Then up a semitone to

- B. Then up a minor 3rd to

- D. Then up a major second to

- E, to start the next octave.

To help your visual memory, follow the movements round the circle as you read the intervals listed above.

Example 10.25: Indicate on the circle the Blues scale on Eb, number the degrees, name the intervals between the scale degrees and indicate its melodic description.

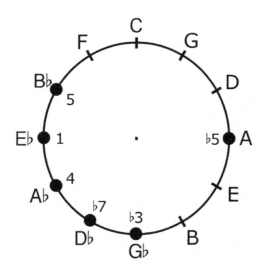

Our set of notes for Eb Blues is Gb, Db, Ab, Eb, Bb, A and in scale order this becomes Eb Gb Ab A Bb Db labeled 1 b3 4 b5 5 b7 by reference to the Eb Major scale.

The intervals involved in the Eb Blues scale are:

- Eb, the tonic, go up a minor 3rd to

- Gb. Then up a major second to

- Ab. Then up a semitone to

- A. Then up a semitone to

- Bb. Then up a minor 3rd to

- Db. Then up a major second to

- Eb, to start the next octave.

To help your visual memory, follow the movements round the circle as you read the intervals listed above.

Notes

11: Chord Scales – Major - Answers

When you review the answers to the examples, take care to follow the explanations note by note on the circle and particularly with the spelling of the chords. This will strengthen your ability to 'see' the intervals which are mainly minor and major thirds up or down when dealing with chords.

Also, be prepared to use enharmonic spellings to avoid double flats or sharps. This will sometimes mean passing from a scale with lots of flats to an enharmonic equivalent with sharps.

The examples in this chapter refer to that part of the content of Chapter 11 of *The Circle of Fifths* which deals with the Major scale.

See the 'Resources' section of this book for the download link for the pack of blank circles to help in your work.

The major scale

Example 11maj.1: You have a chord marked Db. In the harmonization of which major scales could this chord be found? Write the notes of the chord and indicate on the circle on which degrees this chord could be constructed.

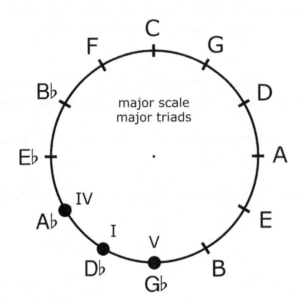

A chord marked simply Db is a perfect major triad (see the conventions in the Introduction) formed from the notes Db, F, Ab. Db is the root note. The illustration above shows the scales in which this chord appears and is to be read as follows:

- Db perfect major triad is built on the tonic, degree I, of the scale Db Major

- Db perfect major triad is built on the dominant, degree V, of the scale Gb Major

- Db perfect major triad is built on the sub-dominant, degree IV, of the scale Ab Major

Note that in this illustration, the degrees IV, I, V are in the reverse order compared with the illustration of scale degrees as in Chapter 2 of *The Circle of Fifths*. In these exercises, we are asking a different question. We are asking on which degrees of which major scale does a particular chord's root note fall.

In the figure above, we are NOT saying that Ab is the IV degree of Db Major. We are saying that on the IV degree of Ab Major we can construct a perfect major triad with root Db.

Example 11maj.2: You have a chord marked A. In the harmonization of which major scales could this chord be found? Write the notes of the chord and indicate on the circle on which degrees this chord could be constructed.

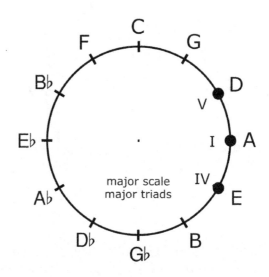

A chord marked simply A is a perfect major triad formed from the notes A, C#, E. A is the root note. The illustration above shows the scales in which this chord appears:

- A perfect major triad is built on the tonic, degree I, of the scale A Major
- A perfect major triad is built on the dominant, degree V, of the scale D Major
- A perfect major triad is built on the sub-dominant, degree IV, of the scale E Major

Example 11maj.3: You have a chord marked F. In the harmonization of which major scales could this chord be found? Write the notes of the chord and indicate on the circle on which degrees this chord could be constructed.

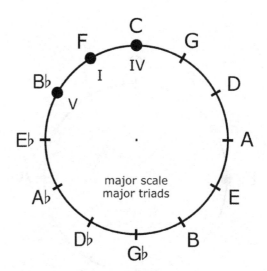

A chord marked simply F is a perfect major triad formed from the notes F, A, C. F is the root note. The illustration above shows the scales in which this chord appears:

- F perfect major triad is built on the tonic, degree I, of the scale F Major
- F perfect major triad is built on the dominant, degree V, of the scale Bb Major
- F perfect major triad is built on the sub-dominant, degree IV, of the scale C Major

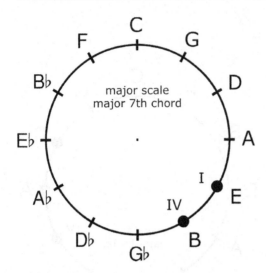

Example 11maj.4: You have a chord marked Emaj7. In the harmonization of which major scales could this chord be found? Write the notes of the chord and indicate on the circle on which degrees this chord could be constructed.

A major seventh chord is one with four notes, consisting of a perfect major triad with a major seventh above the root. In the harmonization of the major scale, major seventh chords are only built on the tonic and sub-dominant degrees.

A chord marked simply Emaj7 is a major seventh chord formed from the notes E, G#, B, D#. E is the root note. The illustration above shows the scales in which this chord appears:

- Emaj7 chord is built on the tonic, degree I, of the scale E Major

- Emaj7 chord is built on the sub-dominant, degree IV, of the scale B Major

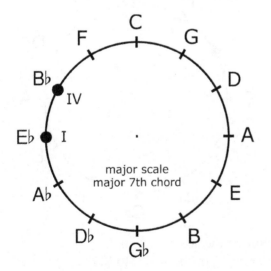

Example 11maj.5: You have a chord marked Ebmaj7. In the harmonization of which major scales could this chord be found? Write the notes of the chord and indicate on the circle on which degrees this chord could be constructed.

A chord marked simply Ebmaj7 is a major seventh chord formed from the notes Eb, G, Bb, D. Eb is the root note. The illustration above shows the scales in which this chord appears:

- Ebmaj7 chord is built on the tonic, degree I, of the scale Eb Major

- Ebmaj7 chord is built on the sub-dominant, degree IV, of the scale Bb Major

Example 11maj.6: You have a chord marked Dmaj7. In the harmonization of which major scales could this chord be found? Write the notes of the chord and indicate on the circle on which degrees this chord could be constructed.

A chord marked simply Dmaj7 is a major seventh chord formed from the notes D, F#, A, C#. D is the root note. The illustration above shows the scales in which this chord appears:

- Dmaj7 chord is built on the tonic, degree I, of the scale D Major
- Dmaj7 chord is built on the sub-dominant, degree IV, of the scale A Major

Example 11maj.7: You have a chord marked D7. In the harmonization of which major scales could this chord be found? Write the notes of the chord and indicate on the circle on which degrees this chord could be constructed.

D7 is the way of indicating a dominant seventh chord sometimes referred to simply as a seventh. It is a chord of four notes, consisting of a perfect major triad with a minor seventh above the root. In the harmonization of the major scale, dominant seventh chords are only built on the dominant, V, degree.

D7 is formed from the notes D, F#, A, C. D is the root note. The illustration above shows the scale in which this chord appears:

- D7 chord is built on the dominant, degree V, of the scale G Major

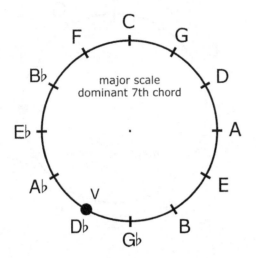

Example 11maj.8: You have a chord marked Ab7. In the harmonization of which major scales could this chord be found? Write the notes of the chord and indicate on the circle on which degrees this chord could be constructed.

Ab7 is formed from the notes Ab, C, Eb, Gb. Ab is the root note. The illustration above shows the scale in which this chord appears:

- Ab7 chord is built on the dominant, degree V, of the scale Db Major

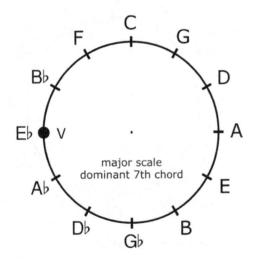

Example 11maj.9: You have a chord marked Bb7. In the harmonization of which major scales could this chord be found? Write the notes of the chord and indicate on the circle on which degrees this chord could be constructed.

Bb7 is formed from the notes Bb, D, F, Ab. Bb is the root note. The illustration above shows the scale in which this chord appears:

- Bb7 chord is built on the dominant, degree V, of the scale Eb Major

Example 11maj.10: You have a chord marked Gm7. In the harmonization of which major scales could this chord be found? Write the notes of the chord and indicate on the circle on which degrees this chord could be constructed.

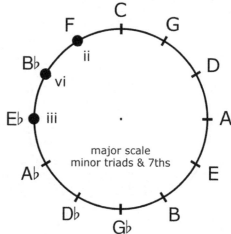

In major scales, when a seventh is added to a minor triad, the result will always be a m7 chord. So examples for minor triads and m7 chords will be the same.

In this example, the Gm7 chord is a perfect minor triad (Gm) with an added minor seventh on top. The notes are: G, Bb, D, F with G being the root note. The illustration above shows the scales in which this chord appears:

- Gm7 chord is built on the second degree, ii, of the scale F Major

- Gm7 chord is built on the sixth degree, vi, of the scale Bb Major

- Gm7 chord is built on the third degree, iii, of the scale Eb Major.

Example 11maj.11: You have a chord marked Ebm7. In the harmonization of which major scales could this chord be found? Write the notes of the chord and indicate on the circle on which degrees this chord could be constructed.

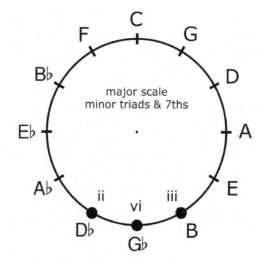

The Ebm7 chord is a perfect minor triad with an added minor seventh on top. The notes are: Eb, Gb, Bb, Db with Eb being the root note. The illustration above shows the scales in which this chord appears:

- Ebm7 chord is built on the second degree, ii, of the scale Db Major

- Ebm7 chord is built on the sixth degree, vi, of the scale Gb Major

- Ebm7 chord is built on the third degree, iii, of the scale Cb Major.

Note that B in the illustration, has been renamed to Cb to comply with the spellings in the scale which has Ebm on the third degree, Cb Major.

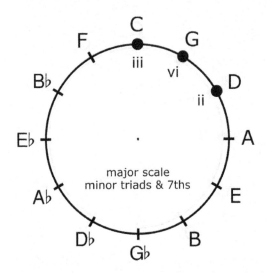

Example 11maj.12: You have a chord marked Em. In the harmonization of which major scales could this chord be found? Write the notes of the chord and indicate on the circle on which degrees this chord could be constructed.

The Em chord is a perfect minor triad. The notes are: E, G, B with E being the root note. The illustration above shows the scales in which this chord appears:

- Em chord is built on the second degree, ii, of the scale D Major

- Em chord is built on the sixth degree, vi, of the scale G Major

- Em chord is built on the third degree, iii, of the scale C Major.

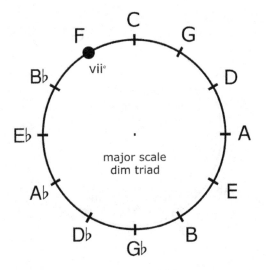

Example 11maj.13: You have a chord marked Edim. In the harmonization of which major scales could this chord be found? Write the notes of the chord and indicate on the circle on which degrees this chord could be constructed.

The Edim chord is a diminished triad. The notes are: E, G, Bb with E being the root note. The illustration above shows the scale in which this chord appears:

- Edim chord is built on the seventh degree, vii, of the scale F Major

Example 11maj.14: You have a chord marked Gdim. In the harmonization of which major scales could this chord be found? Write the notes of the chord and indicate on the circle on which degrees this chord could be constructed.

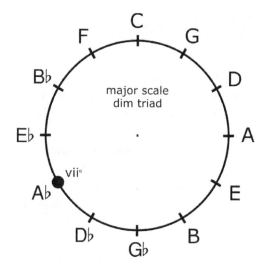

The Gdim chord is a diminished triad. The notes are: G, Bb, Db with G being the root note. The illustration above shows the scale in which this chord appears:

- Gdim chord is built on the seventh degree, vii, of the scale Ab Major

Example 11maj.15: You have a chord marked Am7b5. In the harmonization of which major scales could this chord be found? Write the notes of the chord and indicate on the circle on which degrees this chord could be constructed.

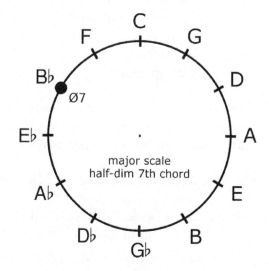

The Am7b5 chord is a half-diminished seventh chord. The notes are: A, C, Eb, G with A being the root note. The illustration above shows the scale in which this chord appears:

- Am7b5 chord is built on the seventh degree, vii, of the scale Bb Major

_ *** _

Your next step

Now that you have completed the exercises which cover chapters 8 through 11 (Major scale part) of *The Circle of Fifths*, continue your musical journey with exercises from Volume 3 of the Workbooks of the Visual Tools for Musicians Series.

The Workbook: Volume 3 – Minor & More is an accessible and straightforward accompanying guide designed to solidify key concepts from Chapters 11 (Minor Scales), 12 and 13 of my best-seller, *The Circle of Fifths: visual tools for musicians*. You'll be encouraged to dive in and develop skills with exercises and additional tutelage. And by following the practical solutions to common pitfalls, you'll soon gain clarity and approach your new passion fearlessly.

In *The Workbook: Volume 3 – Minor & More*, you'll discover:

- **Seventy-eight exercises**, with answers, to convert fledgling know-how into deeply understood notions
- Hands-on training to develop your visualization to grasp the **extra richness** brought by **minor harmony** using examples from the natural, harmonic and ascending melodic minor scales
- A pathway toward relating **quartal harmony** to **pentatonic** and **whole tone** scales enabling you to expand your musicianship by familiarization
- How to visualize the keys required for **transposing instruments** in order to let them join in your group without clashing or **to adapt a new piece of music** for your existing group members.

The Workbook: visual tools for musicians: Volume 3 – Minor & More is the ideal tool for hitting all the right notes. If you like concrete examples, learning through applying principles, and exciting alternative teaching methods, then you'll love my finely tuned handbook.

Get *The Workbook: Volume 3 – Minor & More* to make sound progress today!

Available in eBook, Paperback and Hard Cover versions
from this universal link*:

https://mybook.to/WorkBook3-MinorMore

* the universal link takes you to the Amazon website for
your country

Other Books

If this workbook has been useful for you, please look up some of my other books.

The Series - *Visual Tools For Musicians*

The Circle of Fifths: visual tools for musicians is the first in the **Visual Tools For Musicians** series and will help you discover many more visual methods to help your musical progressions. You can buy it in eBook or print formats at this universal link :

https://mybook.to/CircleOfFifths

Other books in this series are the three companion workbooks providing exercises to assist you to become comfortable employing the techniques learned in *The Circle of Fifths*.

- **The Workbook: Volume 1 – Early Steps** – contains over 60 new exercises with model answers covering chapters 1 through 7 of *The Circle of Fifths*.

Available in print and eBook formats : https://mybook.to/WorkBook1-FirstSteps

- **The Workbook: Volume 2 – Further Steps** – 64 new exercises with model answers covering chapters 8 to 11 (Major scale part) of *The Circle of Fifths*.

Available in print and eBook formats: https://mybook.to/WorkBook2-FurtherSteps

- **The Workbook: Volume 3 – Minor & More** – 78 new exercises with model answers covering chapters 11 (minor scales) through 13 of *The Circle of Fifths*.

Available in print and eBook formats: https://mybook.to/WorkBook3-MinorMore

The whole **Visual Tools for Musicians Series** is available in **Large Print** format https://mybook.to/VisualToolSeriesLP

Notes on Music Theory Series

- **Why Scales Need Sharps and Flats** – a detailed look at the construction of our fundamental reference, the major scale.

Available in print and eBook formats: https://mybook.to/SharpsAndFlats

* the universal links take you to the Amazon website for your country

Resources

The file of blank circles mentioned throughout this workbook is available for download, if you so wish.

The file, Blank-Circles-2023.pdf, has been zipped for download and you can access it via this link:

https://le-theron.com/workbook-v2/

Thank you

Thank you for reading *The Workbook: Volume 2 – Further Steps*. If you have any comments and suggestions, please contact us by email. Your comments will help us to improve later editions. You can contact us by email at :

email : support@le-theron.com

Website : https://le-theron.com

One last thing

Want to help a reader out? Reviews are crucial when it comes to helping readers choose their next book and you can help them by just leaving a few sentences as a review. It doesn't have to be anything fancy, just what you liked about the book and who you think might like to read it.

https://www.amazon.com/review/create-review?&asin=B094DM77C5

Thank you.

— ### —

Made in the USA
Monee, IL
04 October 2023

43975758R00052